MESSI

THE DEFINITIVE STORY OF A FOOTBALL ICON

200+ Entertaining Trivia Questions, Exciting Fun Facts, Untold Inspiring Stories, and Engaging Interactive Activities for Leonel Messi fans everywhere

This book is dedicated to Charlie, Matilda, Asia, Holly, Valerie and Mark

TWO FREE BONUSES !

The most controversial Wold Cup moments ever
The most outragous Premier League moments ever

- What did Maradona really say about his infamous "Hand of God" goal?
- Why did Zidane headbutt Materazzi in a World Cup final?
- Why Eric Cantona hurled a Kung-Fu kick into the crowd?
- What made Paulo Di Canio push the refree onto the ground?
- Why a Columbian player was killed for scoring an own goal?

To find the answers scan the QR code and download your free copies

SCAN ME

CONTENTS

INTRODUCTION

On 20th December 2022, during the penalty shootout in the World Cup final in Qatar, Argentina's Leonel Messi stood on the verge of immortality. Adding the greatest prize in world football to his enormous list of achievements would end the debate that has been raging for years. He would confirm his place as the greatest footballer of all time.

In that monumental moment, with the eyes of the world upon him, Messi humbly looked up to the sky and whispered...

"It could be today grandma".

Luis Lionel Andres Messi was born in Rosario, Argentina in 1987. Hi parents worked in factories to help support him and his three siblings. From a very young age Messi would kick a ball around with his two older brothers. Then at the age of four, his grandmother Celia persuaded the coach of the local club Grimidi, to let him play for the team. Despite being much smaller than the other players, Messi scored two goals and left the coach speechless. "He's like a little flea you cannot shake".

He became a regular in the team and his grandmother would help nurture his talent, taking him to all his games and was a constant source of inspiration and support. After a disagreement with the coaching team at Grimindi, Messi joined the youth team at the local professional side Newell's Old boys where he would play an instrumental role in their 87 team.

At the age of 11 Messi's grandfather passed away. Which had a deeply profound effect on him. From that moment, Messi vowed to pay homage to his late grandmother whenever he could. After every goal he scored he would look to sky and point, honouring the woman who played such a key part in his development and helped him grow his deep passion for the game.

Around the same time Messi, was diagnosed with growth hormone disorder. His treatment would come at a great cost, but fortunately Newell's Old Boys agreed to help finance it. However this did not last long and Messi found himself in a situation where his family were unable to pay for his treatment.

There was some interest from other Argentine clubs, but Messi's family members in Catalonia arranged a trial at the Barcelona FC academy in Spain. After just one match the club were keen to sign the young prodigy.

It was extremely rare for Barcelona to sign such a young player from outside the EU. But Messi's potential was clear to see. Grabbing whatever was at hand, the Barcelona scout gave Messi a napkin, on which he signed his first contract.

At age 13 Messi joined Barcelona's prestigious La Masia academy. This was the perfect place for his talent to be nurtured. As part of the deal the club agreed to fund his continued treatment and provided the family with a home in the city, near the famous Camp Nou stadium.

Messi stood out amongst the group of gifted youngsters and he made his way up through the ranks until he began training with the first team. Ronaldinho, the club's Brazilian superstar told everyone that one day this young man would be even greater than him. Ronaldinho took him under his wing and nicknamed him "little brother".

At the age 16 Messi made his competitive debut for Barcelona against. In his first season he helped Barcelona win the La Liga championship and scored his first goal, assisted by his mentor Ronaldinho. And of course, after scoring, he pointed to the sky to honour his late Grandmother.

Over the following years Messi's grew from a young prodigy into a global superstar. A once in a generation talent that did things on the pitch that seemed at times to be impossible, inhuman, like a PlayStation character in real life. His ability to dribble his way past defenders and create and score goals was uniquely breathtaking. His rivalry with Real Madrid forward Cristiano Ronaldo defined an era. And the statics from both players will be hard to follow.

Messi rewrote the history books, smashing records and redefining the modern game. As the number of domestic and personal accolades grew there was a hole missing. His success on the international stage with Argentina was proving harder to come by. It got to the point where his country blamed him for their lack of trophies and accused him of only caring about club football in Spain.

Then on December 2021 in the Copa America final against Argentina's rivals Brazil, at their home stadium, the Maracana in Rio De Janeiro, Messi finally lifted a trophy for Argentina. The only thing missing from his vast collection of honours was the biggest prize in the football. The FIFA World Cup.

Coming into the 2022 Qatar World Cup it felt like it was written in the stars that Messi would come away with a winners medal around his neck. Things however did get off to a good start. To the surprise of most, Argentina lost their opening game against Saudi Arabia. It felt to many that perhaps this might not be Messi's golden farewell after all.

In the second match Argentina vitally needed a win to stay in the tournament. The game was tense and poised on a knife edge. Then late into the game the great man did what he does best. He scored the winning goal and keep his countries hopes alive.

Argentina qualified from their group and made their way through the lockout stages until they reached the final against France.

After a close and tense match the game finished 3-3 after extra time meaning a dreaded penalty shootout would decide the fate of both nations.

Messi converted his penalty in the shootout and joined his teammates on the halfway line to nervously watch the rest unfold. He looked on as both teams scored their penalties. Then the Argentina goalkeeper made a save, giving them an advantage. Messi looked up to the sky.

Up to his grandmother, the woman who all those years ago had believed in his gift, nurtured his talent and supported his dreams. The women who had set a small boy from Rosario on a journey to becoming the greatest player in the history of the game.

"It could be today Grandma"

Moments later Argentina scored the winning penalty, and as the stadium erupted and the whole of Argentina jumped and screamed with joy, little Leonel Messi fell to his knees and pointed up at the sky.

He was champion of the world.

At last.

This book is more than just a series of trivia questions, puzzles, fun facts, stories and stats. It is a celebration of a football icon. A humble hero who has inspired generations and will continue to do so long after he hangs up his boots in Miami.

Messi is unquestionably the greatest footballer of all time. And over the course of this book you will discover why.

CHAPTER 1

CHILDHOOD

"Messi is the Mozart of soccer."

- Radomir Antic

TRIVIA QUESTIONS

1. **On 24th June of which year was Messi Born?**
   a) 1985
   b) 1986
   c) 1987
   d) 1988

2. **In which city in Argentina was Messi born?**
   a) Rosario
   b) Mendoza
   c) Buenos Aires
   d) Salta

3. **What's his full name?**
   a) Lionel Andres Messi
   b) Luis Lionel Andres Messi
   c) Luis Lionel Messi
   d) Lionel Anderson Messi Blanco

4. **Messi's father, Jorge Messi was a steel factory manager, where did his mother, Celia Cuccittini work?**
   a) A school
   b) A nursery
   c) A magnet manufacturing workshop
   d) A bakery

5. **Messi is known for his incredible dribbling and goalscoring ability. What is his dominant foot?**
   a) Left
   b) Right

6. **Which member of the Messi family discovered his talent and forced a local club to let him play for them?**
   a) Mother
   b) Father
   c) Grandmother
   d) Aunt

7. **How many siblings does Messi have?**
   a) 1
   b) 2
   c) 3
   d) 4

8. **Messi's nickname is "La Pulga". What does it mean?**
   a) Little genius
   b) Little flea
   c) Little feet
   d) Little fly

9. **At the age of 10, Messi was diagnosed with what medical condition?**
   a) Heart disease
   b) growth hormone disorder
   c) Diabetes
   d) leukemia

10. **What was the estimated monthly cost of his treatment?**
    a) $300
    b) $600
    c) $1000
    d) $1500

INTERACTIVE ACTIVITY CHALLENGE

Wordsearch 1

L	R	F	D	Z	X	N	G	D	T	F	Y	K	A	Z	H	Y	I	P	H
D	E	Q	L	W	G	E	L	L	O	R	A	S	Q	I	S	U	J	M	Y
G	A	O	O	F	F	W	S	D	V	T	L	M	A	G	E	B	F	S	O
Z	V	D	H	I	D	E	R	F	E	L	F	D	Z	R	E	W	B	P	J
H	G	F	A	L	F	L	O	E	O	F	E	F	J	A	A	X	D	K	K
C	D	L	Q	F	W	L	D	B	F	K	W	J	K	N	N	K	I	C	O
S	P	K	E	S	V	S	B	I	D	G	I	B	U	D	T	V	L	B	K
N	A	P	K	I	N	O	S	N	X	U	H	P	W	O	K	L	S	G	J
P	H	C	G	A	B	L	H	F	K	H	G	N	J	L	C	J	F	R	O
N	A	C	A	U	H	D	A	G	L	M	E	S	S	I	D	T	F	A	R
X	S	C	Y	E	B	B	F	V	X	Q	G	Z	H	Y	B	R	O	N	Z
B	A	X	R	Y	S	O	G	F	R	O	M	S	U	J	A	S	U	D	E
D	D	P	O	A	D	Y	D	A	J	Z	D	Z	D	C	Q	M	Z	M	J
Z	S	F	S	O	B	S	V	X	C	U	K	I	M	L	F	G	S	O	I
O	S	B	A	R	C	E	L	O	N	A	O	V	J	A	F	S	V	T	C
S	A	Z	R	A	E	B	T	M	R	Y	H	I	K	P	K	J	A	H	A
L	E	S	I	V	J	J	H	G	B	F	A	T	X	U	M	H	X	E	G
P	D	F	O	G	D	N	H	Z	V	J	D	M	L	L	K	L	I	R	M
W	F	J	F	X	X	F	R	E	D	H	X	E	T	G	G	N	H	L	C
D	D	C	Q	A	R	G	E	N	T	I	N	A	L	A	S	A	U	J	J

Find the hidden words

MESSI
ARGENTINA
ROSARIO
GRANDMOTHER
BARCELONA
NEWELLS OLD BOYS
LEO
LA PULGA
NAPKIN
GRANDOLI

ANSWERS

CHAPTER 1: CHILDHOOD

TRIVIA QUESTIONS:

1. c) 1987
2. a) Rosario
3. b) Luis Lionel Andres Messi
4. c) A magnet manufacturing workshop
5. a) Left
6. c) Grandmother
7. c) 3
8. b) Little flea
9. b) growth hormone disorder
10. c) $1000

INTERACTIVE ACTIVITY CHALLENGE: Wordsearch 1

L	R	F	D	Z	X	N	G	D	T	F	Y	K	A	Z	H	Y	I	P	H
D	E	Q	L	W	G	E	L	L	O	R	A	S	Q	I	S	U	J	M	Y
G	A	O	O	F	F	W	S	D	V	T	L	M	A	G	E	B	F	S	O
Z	V	D	H	I	D	E	R	F	E	L	F	D	Z	R	E	W	B	P	J
H	G	F	A	L	F	L	O	E	O	F	E	F	J	A	A	X	D	K	K
C	D	L	Q	F	W	L	D	B	F	K	W	J	K	N	N	K	I	C	O
S	P	K	E	S	V	S	B	I	D	G	I	B	U	D	T	V	L	B	K
N	A	P	K	I	N	O	S	N	X	U	H	P	W	O	K	L	S	G	J
P	H	C	G	A	B	L	H	F	K	H	G	N	J	L	C	J	F	R	O
N	A	C	A	U	H	D	A	G	L	M	E	S	S	I	D	T	F	A	R
X	S	C	Y	E	B	B	F	V	X	Q	G	Z	H	Y	B	R	O	N	Z
B	A	X	R	Y	S	O	G	F	R	O	M	S	U	J	A	S	U	D	E
D	D	P	O	A	D	Y	D	A	J	Z	D	Z	D	C	Q	M	Z	M	J
Z	S	F	S	O	B	S	V	X	C	U	K	I	M	L	F	G	S	O	I
O	S	B	A	R	C	E	L	O	N	A	O	V	J	A	F	S	V	T	C
S	A	Z	R	A	E	B	T	M	R	Y	H	I	K	P	K	J	A	H	A
L	E	S	I	V	J	J	H	G	B	F	A	T	X	U	M	H	X	E	G
P	D	F	O	G	D	N	H	Z	V	J	D	M	L	L	K	L	I	R	M
W	F	J	F	X	X	F	R	E	D	H	X	E	T	G	G	N	H	L	C
D	D	C	Q	A	R	G	E	N	T	I	N	A	L	A	S	A	U	J	J

FUN FACTS, STOIRES AND STATS

Luis Lionel Andres Messi was born on 24th June 1987 in Rosario, Santa Fe, Argentina, he is the third of four children of Jorge Messi, a steel factory manager, and Celia Cuccittini, who worked in a magnet manufacturing workshop.

On his father's side, he is of Spanish and Italian descent. He is the great-grandson of immigrants from the Adriatic Marche region of Italy. He has primarily Italian ancestry on his mother's side.

Growing up in a close-knit, football-loving family, Messi developed a passion for the game from an early age. He used to play constantly with his older brothers, Rodrigo and Matías, as well as his cousins, Maximiliano and Emanuel Biancucchi, who both became professional footballers like Leo.

Messi's three siblings are all very close to their superstar brother. His brother Matías looks very similar to him and they were often mistaken for one another when they were younger. His other brother Rodrigo, was perhaps the most instrumental in getting his brother to play football as a child despite his small size. Rodrigo has continued to play a big part in Messi's career ever since and is now Lionel's manager of public relations who deals with the media and other inquiries. Messi's sister is called Maria Sol Messi and is the brand manager for Messi's fashion store, "The Messi Store"

In 1991, at the age of 4, Messi's grandmother Celia Olivera Cuccittini, convinced the reluctant coach of the local Rosario team, Salvador Aparicio, to let him play in their team, despite being younger and much smaller than their opponents. The team was known as the worst in town and they lost most of the matches they played in so the coach agreed, saying "I'm putting him near the touchline so when he cries you can take him home." The young Messi scored two goals in the match and the coach was stunned, saying that no one could shake him off the ball. He was like a little flea you can't get rid of.

His nickname, "La Pulga", which translates to "little flea", is the nickname that would eventually follow him to Barcelona, where it perfectly describes his ability to dribble through much taller players with pace and precision.

Messi's grandmother was his greatest admirer and his closest aide when he began playing football at such a young age. She took him to all his games and was his inspiration for his early success. She sadly passed away when Messi was aged 11 years old and this had a profound effect on him.

When Messi scores he always makes the same gesture, by looking to the sky and pointing upwards towards the sky with both forefingers. This gesture is thought to be in honor of his grandmother. During the 2022 FIFA World Cup final penalty shootout, Messi was seen by the camera looking to the sky and saying "It could be today grandma".

Rosario, Messi's birthplace, is the third most populated city in Argentina, behind Buenos Aires and Cordoba. It is a riverport, perched on the imposing Parana River. The city has nearly two million inhabitants and it is an important nerve center in the Argentinian economy.

In 2021 a 226-foot-tall mural of Messi's face was painted onto a tower black in Rosario by local artists Marlene Zuriaga and Lisandro Urteaga. It took a month to complete and is titled: "From Another Galaxy And From My City".

CHAPTER 2

YOUTH CAREER

"I have seen the player who will inherit my place in Argentine soccer and his name is Messi. Messi is a genius."

- Diego Maradona

TRIVIA QUESTIONS

1. **What was the name of Messi's first local Rosario team, which he joined at the age of 4 years old?**
   a) Grandoli
   b) Lanús
   c) Chervos
   d) Sintani

2. **At which age did he join his local professional team Newell's Old Boys?**
   a) 5
   b) 6
   c) 7
   d) 8

3. **Aged 11, Newell's ended the season undefeated. How many goals did Messi score?**
   a) 29
   b) 36
   c) 43
   d) 55

4. **Overall Messi scored 234 goals for Newell's Old Boys in how many matches?**
   a) 176
   b) 203
   c) 234
   d) 258

5. **After one trial at Barcelona, what did Lionel Messi sign his first football contract on?**
   a) A football trading card
   b) A paper napkin
   c) An actual football
   d) A Barcelona shirt

6. **At what age did Messi join the Barcelona Youth Academy, La Masia?**
   a) 10
   b) 12
   c) 13
   d) 15

7. **After his second game for the youth team, what did Messi do?**
   a) Scored a hat trick
   b) Scored 6 goals
   c) fractured his fibula
   d) Got sent off

8. **Messi became an integral part of the "Baby Dream Team", Barcelona's greatest-ever youth side. During his first full season, he was the top scorer with how many goals in 31 games?**
   a) 22
   b) 29
   c) 38
   d) 43

9. **Whilst at the La Masia academy which English Premier League club tried to sign him Messi?**
   a) Arsenal
   b) Chelsea
   c) Man United
   d) Liverpool

10. **He played 97 games for the Barcelona youth team, scoring how many goals?**
   a) 79
   b) 89
   c) 96
   d) 105

INTERACTIVE ACTIVITY CHALLENGE

Messi's Maze 1

Find your way out of Messi's maze

ANSWERS

CHAPTER 2: YOUTH CAREER

TRIVIA QUESTIONS:

1. a) Grandoli
2. b) 6
3. d) 55
4. a) 176
5. b) A paper napkin
6. c) 13
7. c) fractured his fibula
8. c) 38
9. a) Arsenal
10. b) 89

INTERACTIVE ACTIVITY CHALLENGE: Messi's Maze 1

FUN FACTS, STOIRES AND STATS

At just 4 years old Messi joined his first club, the local Rosario team Grandoli. He began to show his quality immediately and was doing the kinds of things that he does today but back then the ball came up to his knees. Unfortunately, Messi's time at Grandoli's ended on a sour note. After a falling out between the club and the Messi family, Leo went to play with the youth team at Rosario's local professional side, Newell's Old Boys.

A supporter of Newell's Old Boys, Messi joined the Rosario club at the age of six years old. During the six years he played for them he was part of "The Machine of '87", the near-unbeatable youth side named for the year of their birth. Many of the team from that era are still close friends with Messi and he often travels back to Rosario to see them.

At the age of 11 Messi's future as a professional player was threatened when he was diagnosed with a growth hormone deficiency. He was the average height of an 8-year-old and at first, doctors believed it to be hypophysis, a defect in the pituitary gland which is the organ that controls the release of hormones that are connected to growth and development. After numerous tests, the doctors determined that Messi would need specialist care to restore growth and development to his muscles and bones.

Messi's treatment would come at great financial cost and his father's health insurance covered his growth hormone treatment for two years. At a cost of around $1,000 per month. Newell's Old Boys agreed to contribute to the treatment but later reneged on their promise. He was then scouted by the Buenos Aires club River Plate but they also declined to pay for his treatment.

Messi's family relatives in Catalonia arranged a trial with Barcelona in September 2000. The first team director Charly Rexach was so impressed that he immediately wanted to sign him. However, the club was hesitant due to his size and the rarity of signing a non-EU player for a European club at such a young age. So Messi was sent back home to Argentina.

On 14 December 2000, Messi had a trial with Barcelona. The Messi family threatened to take their child's talent elsewhere. Team executive Carles Rexach saw the potential that the 12-year-old possessed, and he couldn't let him slip away, so he crafted a contract on the spot on a napkin. Messi accepted the makeshift contract, and the rest was history.

In February 2001, with Messi aged 13, the Messi family relocated to Barcelona and moved into an apartment near the club's stadium, the Camp Nou.

On April 7, 2001, Messi played his first official game for the Barcelona youth team and quickly showed why he was such a talent scoring in a 3-0 win against Amposta. However, after several days later everything went wrong again. In his second game, against Tortosa Messi was taken off due to a fractured fibula. He spent four months recovering and then began training with the Under 14 team the following season, but quickly moved up into the Under 16 team. Although he had to wait a few months to play official matches due to bureaucratic issues... he was eventually able to play 10 official matches, scoring nine goals.

During the 2002-03 season, Messi played a pivotal role in Barcelona's "Baby Dream Team". This was in reference to Barcelona's 1992 European Cup-winning side, known as the "Dream Team". While Gerard Pique and Cesc Fabregas, who were also part of the "Baby Dream Team", moved to Manchester United and Arsenal respectively, Messi decided to stay at Barcelona. Years later he would be reunited with both of his former teammates in Barcelona.

The "Baby Dream Team' won an unprecedented treble. They won the league and both the Spanish and Catalan cups. The final of the Copa Catalunya, which Barcelona won 4-1, became known in club lore as the "Partido de la máscara" - "the final of the mask". A week after suffering a broken cheekbone, Messi was forced to play the game wearing a plastic face protector. He soon felt hindered by the mask, so he removed it. He then scored two goals in 10 minutes, before being substituted for his safety.

English Premier League team Arsenal almost signed Messi as a teenager. However, the potential deal broke down because Arsenal was unable to arrange accommodation for Messi and his family, who were all keen for him to join the London club.

CHAPTER 3

BREAKING THROUGH AT BARCELONA

He's an incredible person. Messi is not simply a uniquely talented footballer. He's also strong mentally, very bright, and exceptionally dedicated to his job. Personally speaking, I enjoy watching him play, and I'm deeply proud of him and what he has achieved. Quite simply, he's the best.

- Frank Rijkaard

LFP
10

TRIVIA QUESTIONS

1. **What was Messi's shirt number when he first broke into the Barcelona first team?**
   a) 19
   b) 23
   c) 30
   d) 42

2. **How old was Messi when he made his full debut for Barcelona?**
   a) 16
   b) 17
   c) 18
   d) 19

3. **Against which club was it?**
   a) RCD Espanyol
   b) Real Betis
   c) Real Sociedad
   d) Sevilla

4. **Who was the manager when he made his debut?**
   a) Luis Enrique
   b) Frank Rijkaard
   c) Pep Guardiola
   d) Bobby Robson

5. **Messi scored his first official goal for Barcelona in May 2005, in stoppage time of a game against which club?**
   a) Getafe
   b) Sevilla
   c) Albacete
   d) Cadiz

6. **Which player assisted Messi's goal?**
   a) Ronaldinho
   b) Rivaldo
   c) Xavi
   d) Deco

7. **Against which team did Messi make his UEFA Champions League debut?**
   a) Benfica
   b) Inter Milan
   c) Shakhtar Donestk
   d) Monaco

8. **Who were the opponents when Messi played his first domestic Cup final for Barcelona?**
   a) Athletico Bilbao
   b) Real Madrid
   c) Real Betis
   d) Athletico Madrid

9. **Messi scored his first hat trick for Barcelona, against which club?**
   a) Real Madrid
   b) Athletico Madrid
   c) Valencia
   d) Real Betis

10. **On his 18th birthday signed his first contract as a member of the first team. How much was the buyout clause in it?**
   a) 100m Euros
   b) 125m Euros
   c) 150m Euros
   d) 175m Euros

INTERACTIVE ACTIVITY CHALLENGE

Word Scramble 1

Unscramble the words to find the answers

1. SMSIE ....
2. IGNANERTA ....
3. ORRASIO ....
4. OERAABLNC ....
5. ELYOELONWDLBSS ....
6. NARRHTDMGOE ....
7. LONIROHNDA ....
8. PPE GDAORLUIA ....
9. ANFRK RAAJDIRK ....
10. LEANAOTN ....
11. INAELMAS ANTPONALAI ....
12. LOE ISSEM ONFUTIDANO ....
13. OIHGAT ....
14. LA MAASI ....
15. DORNLGIA ....
16. NNAPIK ....
17. LSRAENA ....
18. EAACETBL ....
19. ELAR MRADID ....
20. IOSICNRTA OLONDRA ....

ANSWERS

CHAPTER 3: BREAKING THROUH AT BARCELONA

TRIVIA QUESTIONS:

1. c) 30
2. b) 17
3. a) RCD Espanyol
4. b) Frank Rijkaard
5. c) Albacete
6. a) Ronaldinho
7. c) Shakhtar Donestk
8. a) Athletico Bilbao
9. a) Real Madrid
10. c) 150m Euros

INTERACTIVE ACTIVITY CHALLENGE: Word Scramble 1

1. MESSI
2. ARGENTINA
3. ROSARIO
4. BARCELONA
5. NEWELLS OLD BOYS
6. GRANDMOTHER
7. RONALDIHNO
8. PEP GUARDIOLA
9. FRANK RIJKAARD
10. ANTONELA
11. MILANESA NAPOLITANA
12. LEO MESSI FOUNDATION
13. THIAGO
14. LA MASIA
15. GRANDOLI
16. NAPKIN
17. ARSENAL
18. ALBACETE
19. REAL MADRID
20. CRISTIANO RONALDO

FUN FACTS, STOIRES AND STATS

On 16th November 2003 at 16 years, four months, and 23 days old, Massi made his first appearance for the Barcelona senior team in a friendly match against former Barcelona assistant manager, Joe Mourinho's FC Porto. He came on a second-half substitute. He was lively from the start and showed his confidence whilst running at defenders. He created two chances and had a shot on goal. The Barcelona staff were delighted with his performance and promoted him to train with the Barcelona B team and have weekly sessions with the first team.

After his first training session with the Barcelona senior squad, the team's star player, the Brazilian Ronaldinho, told his teammates that he believed the 16-year-old Messi would become an even greater player than himself. Ronaldinho soon took Messi under his wing, and referred to him as his "little brother". This greatly eased Messi's transition into the first team.

On October 16th, 2004, made his La Liga debut for Barcelona against city rivals Espanyol. He came on as a substitute replacing Deco in the 82nd minute. At the age of 17 years and three months, Messi became the youngest player ever to represent Barcelona in an official competition.

He was given his debut by the Dutchman Frank Rijkaard, who managed Barcelona from 2003 to 2008. Messi has said that he is the most important coach of his career. He trusted Messi's abilities and he picked him to play for the first team at the right time. If he had got that wrong, who knows where Messi might have been today.

On 1st May 2005, Leo Messi scored his first official goal for Barcelona. It was against Albacete, with a skillful assist from Ronaldinho. Messi came on as a late substitute and immediately made an impact. He soon scored a goal but it was ruled out for offside. Moments later Ronaldinho scooped a pass over a defender and Messi lobbed the ball over the goalkeeper to score the first of many Barcelona goals and at the time, Barcelona's youngest-ever goalscorer in an official competition.

During the 2004/05 season, he played a total of 244 minutes in 9 substitute appearances for the first team and celebrated the first major trophy of his career when Barcelona lifted the La Liga

On his 18th birthday, Messi was rewarded with his first contract as a first-team player. He signed a 5-year contract which included a buyout clause of 150 million euros. Italian side Inter Milan met the buyout clause and offered treble Messi's wages in an attempt to sign the young star. But Messi was not interested and a few months later Barcelona offered him another contract extension, this time until 2014. Which he gladly signed. And the rest is football history.

Messi missed most of the start of the 2005/06 season due to issues with his legal status in the Royal Spanish

Football Federation (RFEF). It was only after acquiring Spanish citizenship on 26 September 2005 that he became eligible to play.

Messi had originally worn the number 30 jersey in his first couple of seasons with the first team. But as he slowly began to establish himself in the starting lineup, he was handed the number 19 jersey. He was the first-choice right-winder in a formidable attacking trio of Samuel Etoo and Ronaldinho.

On March 10th, 2007 in his fourth game against Barcelona's fierce rivals Real Madrid, and at the age of just 19 years old, Messi scored his first hat trick for the club. Having pulled Barcelona level twice, the score stood at 3-2 to Real Madrid in the final minutes of the game. Until Messi leveled the match at 3-3 and took home the match ball. Messi scored an incredible 26 goals in games between Spain's two giants, with 18 of those coming in La Liga games.

MESSI
10
unicef

CHAPTER 4

THE BARCELONA GLORY YEARS

"In my entire life I have never seen a player of such quality and personality at such a young age, particularly wearing the 'heavy' shirt of one of the world's great clubs... Before a game, you can plan for everything. But Messi can produce a move that no-one expects and change the game in an instant."

- Fabio Capello

TRIVIA QUESTIONS

1. **Against which Spanish club did Messi score a near replica of Diego Maradona's wonder goal against England in the 1986 World Cup?**
   a) Getafe
   b) Real Zaragoza
   c) Sporting Gijon
   d) Valencia

2. **How old was Messi when he broke César Rodríguez Álvarez's 60-year record and became Barcelona's all-time leading goalscorer?**
   a) 22
   b) 24
   c) 26
   d) 28

3. **Messi's best goalscoring season for Barcelona was 2011-12. How many goals did he score?**
   a) 42
   b) 57
   c) 64
   d) 73

4. **French newspaper L'Equipe awarded Messi a rare 10/10 rating on two occasions. His first was for Barcelona's victory against Arsenal in April 2010. How many goals did he score in that game?**
   a) 2
   b) 3
   c) 4
   d) 5

5. **Messi's second 10/10 came in 2012 when he became the first player to score five goals in a Champions League game. Who were the unfortunate victims that night?**
   a) Bayer Leverkusen
   b) APOEL FC
   c) FC Basel
   d) FC Porto

6. **He scored his final goal for Barcelona against which team?**
   a) Cleta Vigo
   b) Espanyol
   c) Alaves
   d) Villarreal

7. Messi holds the record for the most games played for Barcelona, with 778. He scored 672 goals in those games. How many assists did he get?
a) 199
b) 239
c) 269
d) 301

8. How many of those 672 goals were headers?
a) 23
b) 38
c) 62
d) 78

9. How many red cards did he receive whilst playing in a Barcelona shirt?
a) 0
b) 1
c) 3
d) 7

10. How many trophies did he win with Barcelona?
a) 26
b) 29
c) 32
d) 35

INTERACTIVE ACTIVITY CHALLENGE

Word Search 2

J	E	Y	D	Z	X	N	G	D	T	F	Y	K	T	Z	H	Y	S	G	J
D	F	A	S	H	D	A	B	U	N	K	F	S	R	I	B	U	F	A	O
G	R	F	S	S	Q	W	S	N	W	T	L	M	O	G	A	B	F	N	R
Z	A	D	L	V	H	A	B	I	K	P	F	D	N	R	L	W	W	T	Z
H	N	K	C	A	L	L	O	C	K	F	E	F	A	A	L	X	X	O	G
C	K	L	Q	K	L	L	D	E	V	K	W	J	L	N	O	K	I	N	O
S	R	K	E	U	V	I	B	F	L	G	I	B	D	D	N	V	L	E	K
N	I	P	K	O	N	K	G	E	J	U	H	P	I	O	D	L	S	L	J
P	J	C	G	J	B	L	H	A	T	A	X	L	N	A	O	J	F	O	O
W	K	N	U	M	B	E	R	T	E	N	S	B	H	N	R	T	F	A	R
X	A	I	P	H	B	B	F	R	E	W	L	K	O	T	G	L	W	R	Z
B	A	J	M	Y	S	O	G	Q	M	K	L	A	X	K	N	O	A	O	E
D	R	F	S	O	D	Y	D	F	G	A	X	L	M	A	D	H	Z	C	J
Z	D	B	P	J	B	F	G	Q	E	N	Z	K	S	A	F	A	J	C	I
H	D	D	K	K	F	L	O	E	O	F	E	F	F	A	S	X	D	U	K
S	F	Z	R	K	E	B	T	M	R	Y	H	I	J	P	K	I	A	Z	A
L	H	C	H	A	M	P	I	O	N	S	L	E	A	G	U	E	A	Z	G
P	D	F	O	L	D	N	H	Z	V	J	D	M	Q	L	K	L	I	O	M
W	F	J	F	X	X	F	R	E	D	H	X	E	T	G	G	N	H	L	C
D	D	C	R	I	S	T	I	A	N	O	R	O	N	A	L	D	O	J	J

Find the hidden words

BALLON D'OR
NUMBER TEN
CHAMPIONS LEAGUE
UNICEF
FRANK RIJKAARD

ANTONELOA ROCCUZZO
LA MASIA
RONALDINHO
CRISTIANO RONALDO
LA LIGA

ANSWERS

CHAPTER 4: THE BARCELONA GLORY YEARS

TRIVIA QUESTIONS:

1. a) Getafe
2. b) 24
3. d) 73
4. c) 4
5. a) Bayer Leverkusen
6. a) Cleta Vigo
7. c) 269
8. a) 23
9. b) 1
10. d) 35

INTERACTIVE ACTIVITY CHALLENGE: Word Search 2

J	E	Y	D	Z	X	N	G	D	T	F	Y	K	T	Z	H	Y	S	G	J
D	F	A	S	H	D	A	B	U	N	K	F	S	R	I	B	U	F	A	O
G	R	F	S	S	Q	W	S	N	W	T	L	M	O	G	A	B	F	N	R
Z	A	D	L	V	H	A	B	I	K	P	F	D	N	R	L	W	W	T	Z
H	N	K	C	A	L	L	O	C	K	F	E	F	A	A	L	X	X	O	G
C	K	L	Q	K	L	L	D	E	V	K	W	J	L	N	O	K	I	N	O
S	R	K	E	U	V	I	B	F	L	G	I	B	D	D	N	V	L	E	K
N	I	P	K	O	N	K	G	E	J	U	H	P	I	O	D	L	S	L	J
P	J	C	G	J	B	L	H	A	T	A	X	L	N	A	O	J	F	O	O
W	K	N	U	M	B	E	R	T	E	N	S	B	H	N	R	T	F	A	R
X	A	I	P	H	B	B	F	R	E	W	L	K	O	T	G	L	W	R	Z
B	A	J	M	Y	S	O	G	Q	M	K	L	A	X	K	N	O	A	O	E
D	R	F	S	O	D	Y	D	F	G	A	X	L	M	A	D	H	Z	C	J
Z	D	B	P	J	B	F	G	Q	E	N	Z	K	S	A	F	A	J	C	I
H	D	D	K	K	F	L	O	E	O	F	E	F	F	A	S	X	D	U	K
S	F	Z	R	K	E	B	T	M	R	Y	H	I	J	P	K	I	A	Z	A
L	H	C	H	A	M	P	I	O	N	S	L	E	A	G	U	E	A	Z	G
P	D	F	O	L	D	N	H	Z	V	J	D	M	Q	L	K	L	I	O	M
W	F	J	F	X	X	F	R	E	D	H	X	E	T	G	G	N	H	L	C
D	D	C	R	I	S	T	I	A	N	O	R	O	N	A	L	D	O	J	J

FUN FACTS, STOIRES AND STATS

Lionel Messi has won 35 major trophies with FC Barcelona, making him the most successful player in the club's history. His trophies include 10 La Liga, seven Copa del Rey, four Champions League, three Fifa Club World Cup, three Uefa Super Cup, and eight Supercopa de Espana.

Messi was only 24 when became Barcelona's leading scorer. He overtook César Rodríguez's 60-year record of 226 with a hat-trick in a 5-3 win over Granada. Messi went on to extend that number by a considerable distance. He ended his Barcelona career with an incredible 672 goals. A record that will no doubt last for many more years to come.

In the 2008-09 season, Pep Guardiola led Barcelona to the first domestic treble in Spanish football history. Messi scored 38 goals as Barcelona played scintillating football throughout the season, winning the Copa del Rey, La Liga, and the UEFA Champions League. This team is regarded as one of the greatest in football history.

Messi scored an astonishing 73 goals in the 2011-12 season, with 50 coming in La Liga - the record in a single La Liga campaign. He scored those 73 goals in 60 games which is an average of 1.26 goals per game. 62 were scored with his left foot, 8 were scored with his right foot and 3 were scored with his head.

During the 2009-10 season, Messi became the only player in history to win the Ballon d'Or, FIFA World Player, Pichichi Trophy (top scorer in La Liga) and Golden Boot in the same season.

Barcelona won their second treble in the 2014-15 season and became the first club to achieve this feat on two separate occasions in Europe. Managed by another ex-Barcelona star, Luis Enrique the team swept all that lay before them. The treble saw them win the European Cup/Champions League as well as the La Liga in the same season for the fifth time. A record across Europe.

The French newspaper L'Equipe has become synonymous over the years with its harsh post-match player ratings. Only 16 performances have been deemed worthy of a 10/10 rating, and Lionel Messi is the only player to have achieved this feat twice. The first came in 2010 when Messi single-handedly demolished Arsenal in the Champions League. He scored four goals and prompted Arsenal manager Arsene Wenger to describe him as "a PlayStation player". Two years later he achieved his second. This time it came in a last-16 match against Bayer Leverkusen. Barcelona won the match 7-1 and Messi scored five goals.

On 23 December 2020, Messi scored his 644th goal for Barcelona. The goal meant that he had surpassed Brazilian legend Pelé's record with Santos as the player with the most goals scored for a single club. To celebrate this achievement, Budweiser sent personalized bottles of beer to every goalkeeper that Messi has scored against.

On 17 January 2021, Messi was sent off for the first and only time in his club career. The red card came in the final minutes of Barcelona's 3-2 extra-time defeat to Athletic Bilbao in the 2020–21 Supercopa de España Final. The card was given for violent conduct after he swung an arm at the head of Asier Villalibre. The incident was initially missed by VAR but subsequently given after further inspection.

Messi made 149 appearances in the Champions League for Barcelona, scoring 120 times and getting 36 assists. He won the trophy three times. Twice as part of the Barcelona treble-winning sides and once in 2011.

CHAPTER 5

MESSI AT PSG

"He's the only player I've met who runs faster with the ball than without."

- Pep Guardiola

TRIVIA QUESTIONS

1. **In which year did Messi sign for PSG?**
   a) 2019
   b) 2020
   c) 2021
   d) 2022

2. **How much did Paris Saint Germain pay Barcelona for him?**
   a) A free transfer
   b) £45 million
   c) £65 million
   d) £100 million

3. **What jersey number did he wear?**
   a) 10
   b) 14
   c) 32
   d) 30

4. **He made his PSG debut against which team?**
   a) Monaco
   b) Olympic Marselle
   c) Reims
   d) Nantes

5. **Against which team in the UEFA Champions League did Messi score his first goal for PSG?**
   a) Bayern Munich
   b) Manchester City
   c) Real Madrid
   d) Napoli

6. **He got a hatrick of assists in PSG's 3-1 win against which team?**
   a) Nice
   b) Metz
   c) Saint Etienne
   d) Lens

7. **In Messi's final season with PSG, he ended with the highest number of assists in the league with how many?**
   a) 10
   b) 12
   c) 16
   d) 19

8. **He made 75 appearances for PSG, how many goals did he score?**
   a) 24
   b) 32
   c) 29
) 41

9. How many assists did he get?

a) 15
b) 21
c) 28
d) 35

10. How many trophies did he win at PSG?

a) 0
b) 1
c) 2
d) 3

INTERACTIVE ACTIVITY CHALLENGE

Word Scramble 2

Unscramble the words to find the answers

1. YURANGH ....
2. RTTHIY ....
3. NENETNEI ....
4. NET ....
5. BERAY LSEEUKNREV ....
6. AL LGIA ....
7. EQEPUIL ....
8. AMOSIHNCP AULEGE ....
9. LDWRO CUP ....
10. OCAP ACRAEIM ....
11. OELNGD EOHS ....
12. BONALL ROD ....
13. NITRE MIIAM ....
14. ASIPR ASNTI EGIMNAR ....
15. LE SCOSLCIA ....
16. NOU MPCA ....
17. IDAVD EMBAKHC ....
18. LCOIYPM LGDO DALME ....
19. AERYB TMEA ....
20. FNUCEI ....

ANSWERS

CHAPTER 5: MESSI AT PSG

TRIVIA QUESTIONS:

1. c) 2021
2. a) A free transfer
3. d) 30
4. c) Reims
5. b) Manchester City
6. c) Saint Etienne
7. c) 16
8. b) 32
9. d) 35
10. d) 3

INTERACTIVE ACTIVITY CHALLENGE: Word Scramble 2

1. HUNGARY
2. THIRTY
3. NINETEEN
4. TEN
5. BAYER LEVERKUSEN
6. LA LIGA
7. L'EQUIPE
8. CHAMPIONS LEAGUE
9. WORLD CUP
10. COPA AMERICA
11. GOLDEN SHOE
12. BALLON D'OR
13. INTER MIAMI
14. PARIS SAINT GERMAIN
15. EL CLASSICO
16. NOU CAMP
17. DAVID BECKHAM
18. OLYMPIC GOLD MEDAL
19. YERBA MATE
20. UNICEF

FUN FACTS, STOIRES AND STATS

Messi entered the summer of 2021 as a free agent at Barcelona. It was believed that it would only be a matter of time before the club would offer him a new contract. However, that changed when the club's financial problems emerged. La Liga rules state that clubs can only spend a certain amount of their revenue on signing players and paying their salaries. Barcelona's revenue had dropped significantly due to the global pandemic and even with Messi reportedly willing to half his salary, the Catalan giants did not have enough of a wage budget left to offer Messi a new contract. Meaning their golden boy was free to leave the club.

After global hysteria and massive speculation about where he would go next, on 10 August 2021, Messi joined French champions Paris Saint-Germain (PSG). He signed a two-year contract until June 2023 with an option for an extra year.

Messi chose to wear the number 30 jersey because this was the squad number he wore as a teenager when he made his senior debut for Barcelona.

Messi made his debut for the club in a La Liga match on 29th August 2021, coming on as a substitute in the second half of a 2-0 away win against Reims. He made his Champions League debut on 15th September the club in a 1-1 away draw against Club Brugge. Four days later, Messi made his home debut for PSG in a 2-1 win over Lyon.

On 28 September 2021, he scored his first goal for the club, a beautifully curled strike from the edge of the 18-yard box in a 2-0 win against former manager, Pep Guardiola's Manchester City.

On 2 May 2023, Messi was suspended by the club for two weeks and fined. This was due to him taking an unauthorized trip to Saudi Arabia with his family as part of a promotional commercial agreement, resulting in him missing a training session following a 3-1 defeat to Lorient

Several PSG supporters demanded his exit from the club, viewing his absence from training as evidence that he was not willing to fight for the team. They saw this disconnect between themselves and the club's identity.

Messi eventually made a public apology to the club and his teammates for his trip, claiming he thought he had a free day after the match against Lorient.

On 28 May 2023, Messi scored in a 1-1 draw against Strasbourg which handed the Ligue 1 championship title to PSG, the 11th in the club's history and his second in a row. In the process, Messi became the player with the most goals in the history of Europe's top five leagues, with 496 goals. One more goal than his rival Cristiano Ronaldo

Messi's time at PSG did not end with the same positivity as it began. After failing to win the Champions League with the club, Messi and his former Barcelona teammate Neymar came under fire from large sections of the club's fanbase. Towards the end of their time in Paris both players were regularly booed by the fans. Both players decided it was time to leave. With Neymar moving to the Saudi League to play for Al Hilal SFC, Messi making his way to the MLS with Inter Miami.

CHAPTER 6

MESSI AT INTER MIAMI

"I can tell you that I am very happy with the decision we made, not only for the game, for how it is going, but for my family, for how we live day by day, for how we enjoy the city, for this new experience and the reception of the people that was extraordinary from the first day, not only in Miami,"

- Leonel Messi

TRIVIA QUESTIONS

1. **How many people attended Messi's unveiling at the DVR PNK Stadium in Fort Lauderdale?**
   a) 10,000
   b) 15,000
   c) 20,000
   d) 25,000

2. **Which famous England football is co-owner of Inter Miami?**
   a) Wayne Rooney
   b) David Beckham
   c) Bobby Charlton
   d) Harry Kane

3. **Messi scored a last-minute winning goal on his debut against which team in the Leagues Cup?**
   a) Cruz Azul
   b) New York Red Bulls
   c) LA Galaxy
   d) Toronto FC

4. **What shirt number does he wear?**
   a) 10
   b) 23
   c) 32
   d) 30

5. **How much will Messi earn per year?**
   a) $20m
   b) $30
   c) $40
   d) $60

6. **What special clause is written into his contract?**
   a) A stand will be named after him
   b) An ownership stake in the club when he retires
   c) $1m goal bonus
   d) $10 bonus for reaching the playoffs

7. **Inter Miami beat Nashville to win the Leagues Cup, Messi's first trophy in North America. What was the score on penalties after the game ended 1-1 after 90 minutes?**
   a) 5-4
   b) 6-5
   c) 8-7
   d) 10-9

8. **He made his MLS regular season debut against which side?**
   a) New York Red Bulls
   b) Chicago Fire FC
   c) Nashville SC
   d) FC Cincinnati

9. In Messi's first 11 games for Inter Miami, Messi made 8 assists and scored how many goals?
a) 7
b) 9
c) 11
d) 13

10. Which of these celebrities has NOT watched Messi play live for Inter Miami?
a) Prince Harry
b) Jay Z
c) Leonardo DiCaprio
d) Kim Kardashian

INTERACTIVE ACTIVITY CHALLENGE

Word Search 3

J	E	Y	D	Z	X	N	G	D	T	A	X	K	T	Z	T	Y	L	J	J
D	F	P	E	P	G	U	A	R	D	I	O	L	A	H	H	C	J	L	O
G	R	N	L	A	O	B	Y	Q	W	R	F	M	N	O	R	O	N	D	R
Z	M	L	B	R	S	X	W	K	A	D	B	D	A	P	O	I	G	K	Z
H	E	K	Y	I	H	I	D	A	V	I	D	B	E	C	K	H	A	M	G
C	S	R	L	S	W	T	N	S	D	N	Z	J	H	O	E	E	V	S	O
S	S	I	J	S	L	S	G	A	S	T	C	B	D	P	L	F	L	W	K
N	I	N	A	A	F	F	O	E	J	E	F	P	T	A	D	T	A	O	J
P	F	H	N	I	S	F	T	H	V	R	X	L	D	A	Y	S	G	R	O
W	O	O	T	N	E	B	B	B	C	M	I	B	Y	M	K	J	A	L	R
X	U	P	K	T	H	A	R	K	L	I	Q	L	T	E	B	F	N	D	Z
B	N	F	A	G	H	A	C	R	D	A	F	G	V	R	Y	W	H	C	E
D	D	U	S	E	D	Y	T	J	W	M	X	L	K	I	U	A	O	U	J
Z	A	D	P	R	B	L	A	T	A	I	I	A	S	C	F	A	J	P	I
H	T	J	K	M	F	L	O	E	R	H	E	F	F	A	A	X	D	F	K
S	I	T	H	A	U	J	L	G	L	I	R	T	E	L	L	I	A	D	A
L	O	K	H	I	M	G	H	A	I	Q	C	D	E	Q	I	A	A	A	X
P	N	O	O	N	D	H	D	P	Z	C	V	K	W	F	K	L	N	O	K
W	N	M	A	J	O	R	L	E	A	G	U	E	S	O	C	C	E	R	W
D	D	M	S	N	S	X	I	G	O	L	D	E	N	S	H	O	E	G	J

Find the hidden words

MESSI FOUNDATION
COPA AMERICA
GOLDEN SHOE
HATRICK
PEP GUARDIOLA
INTER MIAMI
PARIS SAINT GERMAIN
WORLD CUP
DAVID BECKHAM
MAJOR LEAGUE SOCCER

ANSWERS

CHAPTER 6: MESSI AT INTER MIAMI

TRIVIA QUESTIONS:

1. c) 20,000
2. b) David Beckham
3. a) Cruz Azul
4. a) 10
5. d) $60
6. b) An ownership stake in the club when he retires
7. d) 10-9
8. a) New York Red Bulls
9. c) 11
10. b) Jay Z

INTERACTIVE ACTIVITY CHALLENGE: Word Search 3

J	E	Y	D	Z	X	N	G	D	T	A	X	K	T	Z	T	Y	L	J	J
D	F	P	E	P	G	U	A	R	D	I	O	L	A	H	H	C	J	L	O
G	R	N	L	A	O	B	Y	Q	W	R	F	M	N	O	R	O	N	D	R
Z	M	L	B	R	S	X	W	K	A	D	B	D	A	P	O	I	G	K	Z
H	E	K	Y	I	H	I	D	A	V	I	D	B	E	C	K	H	A	M	G
C	S	R	L	S	W	T	N	S	D	N	Z	J	H	O	E	E	V	S	O
S	S	I	J	S	L	S	G	A	S	T	C	B	D	P	L	F	L	W	K
N	I	N	A	A	F	F	O	E	J	E	F	P	T	A	D	T	A	O	J
P	F	H	N	I	S	F	T	H	V	R	X	L	D	A	Y	S	G	R	O
W	O	O	T	N	E	B	B	B	C	M	I	B	Y	M	K	J	A	L	R
X	U	P	K	T	H	A	R	K	L	I	Q	L	T	E	B	F	N	D	Z
B	N	F	A	G	H	A	C	R	D	A	F	G	V	R	Y	W	H	C	E
D	D	U	S	E	D	Y	T	J	W	M	X	L	K	I	U	A	O	U	J
Z	A	D	P	R	B	L	A	T	A	I	I	A	S	C	F	A	J	P	I
H	T	J	K	M	F	L	O	E	R	H	E	F	F	A	A	X	D	F	K
S	I	T	H	A	U	J	L	G	L	I	R	T	E	L	L	I	A	D	A
L	O	K	H	I	M	G	H	A	I	Q	C	D	E	Q	I	A	A	A	X
P	N	O	O	N	D	H	D	P	Z	C	V	K	W	F	K	L	N	O	K
W	N	M	A	J	O	R	L	E	A	G	U	E	S	O	C	C	E	R	W
D	D	M	S	N	S	X	I	G	O	L	D	E	N	S	H	O	E	G	J

FUN FACTS, STOIRES AND STATS

Lionel Messi-mania has gripped the United States ever since he announced to the world his decision to sign for Inter Miami and play in the USA in the MLS (Major League Soccer). After deciding to leave PSG Messi turned down lucrative offers from Saudi Arabian clubs including Al-Hilal. He has considered a move back to his beloved club Barcelona however that proved financially impossible. His arrival had an immediate impact and not only did home tickets at Inter Miami sell out immediately, but at stadiums across the country the games against Inter Miami did too.

His arrival represents a major coup for co-owner David Beckham's Inter Miami side and for MLS as a whole. His arrival is expected to take the sport of Soccer to new heights in the United States. David Beckham himself played for MLS side LA Galaxy between 2007 - 2012 and had always had a dream of growing the sport in the States. He was dedicated to bringing Messi out to Miami and was in negotiations for almost three years to secure his signature.

The Argentinian signed a deal reportedly worth around $150 million, including an annual salary of $60 million, that lasts through the 2025 MLS season. His yearly salary is supplemented by the guarantee that he will be part of the organization's ownership when he retires. He'll also get a slice of the profits from MLS's broadcasting deal with Apple TV and the Inter Miami team kit sales from Adidas. Once he retires he also has the option to buy another MLS team for $25million.

Messi got off to the perfect start with Inter Miami. He made his debut against Cruz Azul in a Leagues Cup match. He was substituted onto the field eight minutes into the second half with Miami trailing 1-0. The first Inter Miami goal of the new Messi era was scored by Robert Taylor to make the score 1-1. Then in the 94th minute, he scored a free-kick-winning goal and perfectly introduced himself to his new home in the United States.

Messi's arrival in the US has seen a frenzy of celebrities rushing to attend matches. Amongst them are star athletes, Hollywood actors and actresses, famous musicians, and other notable personalities. Names have included LeBron James, Selena Gomez, Prince Harry, Megan Markle, Magic Johnson, Serena Williams, Kim Kardashian, Leonardo DiCaprio and Liam Gallagher.

On 19th August 2023 in front of a packed crowd at Geodis Park, Inter Miami won the Leagues Cup, beating Nashville SC 10-9 on penalties after the teams finished 90 minutes level at 1-1. Messi scored in 90 minutes and also converted his penalty in the shootout. This was Messi's first trophy for Inter Miami.

Messi was given team captaincy as soon as he arrived at the club. This would usually mean that he would lift the trophy after the team won the Leagues Cup. However, he decided to share that moment with former club captain, and USA international, DeAndre Yedlin. It was the ultimate sign of respect.

Messi's long-awaited Major League Soccer debut came on Saturday 26th August against the New York Red Bulls at the Red Bull Arena in Harrison, New Jersey. Coming on as a substitute in the 60th minute, Messi scored Miami's second goal to seal the 2-0 win.

Before Messi's arrival, Inter Miami were winless in their previous 10 games. But in a few short weeks, the Argentinian superstar helped change the trajectory of the club. In his first 11 games for the club, he scored 11 goals, made 8 assists, and won the League Cup.

The club has taken Messi's safety very seriously and provided him with a personal bodyguard. The bodyguard gained widespread attention when videos of his dedicated protection of Messi during Inter Miami games appeared on social media platforms. His name is Yassine Chueko and he is an ex-Navy Seal who fought in Iraq. He takes no prisoners and can be seen marching up and down the touchline at matches, ready to pounce on any threat that might arise.

CHAPTER 7

INTERNATIONAL CAREER

"Failure is often part of the journey and learning, and without disappointments it is impossible for success to come."

- Leonel Messi

TRIVIA QUESTIONS

1. **Against which team did he make his international debut in 2005?**
   a) Brazil
   b) Hungary
   c) Sweden
   d) France

2. **What happened 44 seconds into his debut?**
   a) He scored
   b) He was sent off
   c) He assisted Hernan Crespo
   d) He scored an own goal

3. **In 2010, Messi became Argentina's youngest-ever captain. How old was he?**
   a) 21
   b) 22
   c) 23
   d) 24

4. **On 1st March 2006, Messi scored his first international goal in his sixth appearance for Argentina. It was a friendly match against who?**
   a) Brazil
   b) Paraguay
   c) Moldova
   d) Croatia

5. **How many appearances has he made at the FIFA World Cup?**
   a) 21
   b) 23
   c) 25
   d) 26

6. **In how many of those matches was he awarded the "Man of the Match" award?**
   a) 6
   b) 8
   c) 11
   d) 15

7. **Who did Messi surpass as Argentina's all-time leading scorer in the 2016 Copa America semi-final?**
   a) Diego Maradona
   b) Gabriel Batistuta
   c) Hernan Crespo
   d) Sergio Agüero

8. **Under which manager did Messi help Argentina to Olympic gold in Beijing in 2008?**
   a) Sergio Batista
   b) Diego Maradona
   c) Lionel Scaloni
   d) José Pékerman

9. **On February 25, 2023, Messi lifted the Copa America after beating which team?**
   a) Brazil
   b) Chile
   c) Colombia
   d) Uruguay

10. **Messi finally won the World Cup in 2022 after beating France in the final. How many goals did he score in the tournament?**
   a) 4
   b) 5
   c) 7
   d) 8

INTERACTIVE ACTIVITY CHALLENGE

Messi's Maze 2

Find your way out of Messi's maze

ANSWERS

CHAPTER 7: INTERNATIONAL CAREER

TRIVIA QUESTIONS:

1. b) Hungary
2. b) He was sent off
3. b) 22
4. d) Croatia
5. d) 26
6. c) 11
7. b) Gabriel Batistuta
8. a) Sergio Batista
9. a) Brazil
10. c) 7

INTERACTIVE ACTIVITY CHALLENGE: Messi's Maze 2

FUN FACTS, STOIRES AND STATS

Messi made his international debut for Argentina against Hungry on August 17th, 2005 at the age of 18. The game did not go as he had hoped. The youngster had been called into Jose Pekerman's squad for the first time after an impressive showing in the recent Under-20 World Championships. He came on as a 64th-minute substitute and 44 seconds later, whilst attempting to dribble past Vilmos Vanczak, Messi was fouled and immediately retaliated. Moments later, to the shock of everyone in the stadium, Messi was sent off. Messi was reportedly found weeping in the dressing room after his sending-off.

Since Messi has lived in Spain since he was 13 years old., Messi has dual nationality and qualified to play for Spain when he was younger. In 2004 he was asked to play for the Spanish Under 20 side but turned down the opportunity. A year later he led the Argentina Under 20 side to victory in the FIFA Youth Championship.

On 1 March 2006, during Messi's sixth appearance for his country, he scored his first international goal. It came in a friendly match against Croatia. Messi stole the ball of a defender on the right wing then nimbly cut inside and dribbled infield before curling the ball into the bottom left corner. Argentina lost the match 3-2 but Messi's journey to becoming his country's time leading scorer had begun.

During the 2006 World Cup in Germany, Messi became

the youngest player to represent Argentina at a FIFA World Cup when he came on as a substitute in the 74th minute in Argentina's second group game against Serbia and Montenegro. Argentina won the match 6-0 and Messi got an assist and scored the sixth goal, making him the sixth-youngest goalscorer in the history of the World Cup.

He did not play in the quarter-final of the 2006 World Cup against Germany, a match in which Argentina were knocked out 4–2 in a penalty shootout. Back home in Argentina, the manager Pékerman's decision to leave Messi on the bench led to widespread criticism. People believed Messi would have changed the outcome of the match in Argentina's favor.

Ahead of the 2008 Summer Olympics, Barcelona legally forbid Messi from playing for Argentina at the tournament because it coincided with the club's Champions League qualifying matches. However, the newly appointed Barcelona manager Pep Guardiola, who had won the tournament with Spain in 1992, forced teh club to change their mind. They agreed and Messi was permitted to join Sergio Batista's under-23 squad in Beijing. Argentina went on to win the Gold medal, beating Nigeria 1-0 in the final.

In 2012 Messi scored a total of 12 goals in 9 games for Argentina. This equaled the record held by Gabriel Batistuta for the most goals scored in a calendar year for Argentina. Then on 21st June 2016, Messi scored his 55th international goal in Argentina's Copa America semi-final win over the United States to become his country's all-time top goalscorer. Gabriel Batistuta had previously held the record with 54 international goals, ahead of Sergio Aguero with 42. It took Messi 111 games to reach this record.

Messi has played in Three Copa America finals. The first came in 2007 when Argentina faced Brazil in the final in Venezuela. It would end in defeat for Mess as Argentina were beaten 3-0 by a strong Brazil side. His second final came in 2016 when Argentina faced Chile in Chile. Again Messi would taste defeat after Argentina lost 4-1 on penalties after a 0-0 draw in 90 minutes. Messi was the only Argentine player to score their penalty in the shootout. His third final was in 2021 against Brazil at the Maracana Stadium in Rio de Janeiro, Brazil. Argentina won the match 1-0 and it was Argentina's first major title since 1993 and Lionel Messi finally lifted his first major trophy for his beloved national team.

Coming into the 2022 Qatar World Cup Argentina was not seen as the favorites, but many neutral fans across the globe were willing Messi to succeed. Many believed that if he were to win the biggest prize in world football then the Messi vs Ronaldo debate would finally be put to rest. Argentina got off to the worst possible start by losing 2-1 to Saudi Arabia, despite taking the lead after a Messi penalty early in the match. The Argentina team won their next two games and qualified for the knockout stages where they made their to the final after wins against Australia, The Netherlands, and Croatia. In the final, they faced the World Cup holders France. The two PSG superstars Messi and Mbappe would face off in the final that proved to be one of the greatest ever. Argentina took a two-goal lead after a penalty from Messi and a goal from Ángel Di María. Then two late goals from Mbappe tied the match at 2-2 in 90 minutes. In the first half of added time, Messi scored to give Argentina a 3-2 lead before Mbappe completed his hatrick to level the game at 3-3. The match went to penalties and after Messi converted his, and some theatrics from the Argentine goalkeeper, Argentina won the shootout 4-2 and Messi became a World Champion.

By winning the Golden Ball award at the 2022 World Cup, Lionel Messi became the first and only player in history to date to win the award twice. Earlier he had won it at the 2014 World Cup.

CHAPTER 8

MESSI vs RONALDO

"Cristiano had to work and prepare himself to be the best, while for Leo it comes naturally. Those are the greatest differences that I see between the two best players on the planet. Messi plays another sport. For Messi to score three goals [in any given game] is normal."

- Carlos Tevez

5. **Who's first Ballon d'Or was won by a record vote?**
   a) Messi
   b) Ronaldo

6. **Who did Pele say was the better player because of their consistency?**
   a) Messi
   b) Ronaldo

7. **Who won the Champions League first?**
   a) Messi
   b) Ronaldo

8. **Who is the all-time top goalscorer in the Champions League?**
   a) Messi
   b) Ronaldo

9. **Who has an Olympic gold medal?**
   a) Messi
   b) Ronaldo
   c) Both

10. **Who has scored more goals for their country?**
    a) Messi
    b) Ronaldo

INTERACTIVE ACTIVITY CHALLENGE

Crossword 1

Answer the questions to complete the challenge

ACROSS

2. Messi's jersey number when he made his debut for Barcelona
4. Barcelona's academy
5. His first club
9. Barcelona player who called him "Little brother"
10. the number of times Messi has won the ballon d'Or

DOWN

1. His biggest rival
3. Messi's nickname
6. Messi's home country
7. City of Messi's birth
8. Messi's MLS team

ANSWERS

CHAPTER 8: MESSI vs RONALDO

TRIVIA QUESTIONS:

1. a) Messi
2. a) Messi
3. b) Ronaldo
4. b) Ronaldo
5. b) Ronaldo
6. b) Ronaldo
7. a) Messi
8. b) Ronaldo
9. a) Messi
10. b) Ronaldo

INTERACTIVE ACTIVITY CHALLENGE: Cross Word 1

FUN FACTS, STOIRES AND STATS

The Messi versus Ronaldo rivalry has been the greatest of a generation. Arguably it's the greatest ever. Both have very similar records and sporting successes. They spent nine seasons in the prime of their careers regularly facing off while playing for rival clubs Barcelona and Real Madrid.

Both are considered two of the greatest players of all time and have achieved massive historical milestones on the pitch. They are two of the most decorated footballers ever, having won a combined 79 official trophies. Messi leads the way with 44, Ronaldo has 35. They regularly smashed the 50-goal-a-season barrier and fought for domestic and European success with their clubs.

Throughout their rivalry, the pair have dominated awards ceremonies and broken a multitude of goalscoring records for both club and country. Their achievements have been extraordinary. Unlike other historical rivalries, their rivalry has been based on records and reputation, rather than one based on personal loathing. Neither would admit to being friends, but there has always been a mutual respect for one another. Both have been quoted as saying that they thrived off it and used it as fuel to push themselves forward towards unprecedented success.

Between 2009 to 2018, the two faced each other at least twice per season during El Clásico (Barcelona vs Real

Madrid) matches. They also met many other times in other domestic competitions like the Copa del Rey, and the Supercopa de España. In 2011 they both faced off in a two-legged Champions League semi-final. Barcelona won the tie 3-1 after two goals from Messi at the Santiago Bernabéu Stadium.

This period was the most competitive in El Clásico history, both players were their clubs' all-time top scorers. Both players alternated as top scorers in La Liga and the Champions League during most of those seasons whilst both battling for the Ballon d'Or.

The Ballon d'Or award is an annual football award for the best player over the previous calendar year. It was first awarded to Stanley Matthews in 1956 and since then the best players in the world have competed for it. Ronaldo holds the record for most Ballon d'Or nominations with 18 while Messi is the second most-nominated footballer with 15. Ronaldo was the first to win the converted prize in 2008 whilst playing for Manchester United. Messi then won the next four. In total Ronaldo has Five awards and Messi has Seven.

Both Messi and Ronaldo have also been nominated a record 11 times for the UEFA Men's Player of the Year Award. Ronaldo has won this award three times and Messi twice.

As of 2023, Messi and Ronaldo are the only two players to score over 800 goals each in their careers for club and country. It is Ronaldo who holds the record for most official goals in a career with 851 in total. Messi has 819. With both still playing this can easily change.

Most journalists, pundits, and fans agree that these two are the best players of their generation. And many will debate that they are also the greatest of all time. Sighting the individual merits of both players. Ronaldo has received praise for his physical attributes, goalscoring ability, leadership skills, and performance under pressure, as well as his mentality to work harder than everyone else to continuously improve himself. Messi has often been described as a "freak of nature" an anomaly, a once-in-a-lifetime unique genius. He has been praised for his combination of dribbling, playmaking, passing, and goalscoring.

The debate was always going to be settled on their international success because both players have achieved everything there is to achieve at the club level. In 2016 Ronaldo led his Portugal team to victory in the European Championships. The first in the club's history. For many at the time, this was seen as tipping the scales towards Ronaldo. However, in 2021, Messi matched this achievement by helping Argentina lift the Copa America. Then he lifted the 2022 FIFA World Cup, resulting in several football critics, commentators, and players agreeing that the debate was settled, Messi stands alone as the Greatest of all time.

CHAPTER 9

FAMILY AND CHARITY

"For the world of soccer, Messi is a treasure because he is a role model for children around the world... Messi will be the player to win the most Ballons d'Or in history. He is incomparable. He's in a different league."

- Johan Cruyff

TRIVIA QUESTIONS

1. **In which year did Messi marry his long-term partner Antonela Roccuzzo?**
   a) 2008
   b) 2012
   c) 2017
   d) 2020

2. **Who was Messi's best man at the wedding?**
   a) Sergio Aguaro
   b) Cesc Fabregas
   c) His son Thiago
   d) Pep Guariola

3. **How many sons does he have?**
   a) 1
   b) 2
   c) 3
   d) 4

4. **One of Messi's favorite meals is what?**
   a) Tacos
   b) Milanesa Napolitana
   c) Empanadas
   d) Ceviche

5. **What is Messi's favorite drink, which he can often be seen drinking before training sessions?**
   a) yerba mate
   b) Guaraná
   c) El Submarino
   d) Corn Ulpada

6. **He has a tattoo of whom on his left shoulder?**
   a) His son Thiago's face
   b) His mother's face
   c) His Grandmother's face
   d) His wife's face

7. **Messi is the goodwill ambassador for which UN body?**
   a) UNICEF
   b) WHO
   c) UNESCO
   d) PETA

8. **When was the Leo Messi Foundation created?**
   a) 2006
   b) 2007
   c) 2009
   d) 2012

9. **Who runs the foundation?**
   a) His wife
   b) Mother and father
   c) Mother and sister
   d) Mother and brother

10. **Jeweller Ginza Tanaka created a golden cast of his left foot, which was auctioned off for charity. How much was it worth?**
    a) £500
    b) £7500
    c) £1.2 million
    d) £3.5 million

INTERACTIVE ACTIVITY CHALLENGE

Messi's Maze 3

Find your way out of Messi's maze

ANSWERS

CHAPTER 9: FAMILY AND CHARITY

TRIVIA QUESTIONS:

1. c) 2017
2. c) His son Thiago
3. c) 3
4. b) Milanesa Napolitana
5. a) yerba mate
6. b) His mother's face
7. a) UNICEF
8. b) 2007
9. d) Mother and brother
10. d) £3.5 million

INTERACTIVE ACTIVITY CHALLENGE:

FUN FACTS, STOIRES AND STATS

Antonela Roccuzzo was born on 26th February 1988, in Rosario, Santa Fe, Argentina. She has known Messi since she was five years old because her cousin, Lucas Scaglia, was a childhood friend of his. She attended Universidad del Rosario, where she studied dentistry and then social communication before moving to Barcelona to live with Messi.

Messi and Antonela have been in a relationship since 2008. After keeping their relationship private for a year, Messi confirmed their romance in an interview before being seen in public for the first time during a carnival in Sitges after a Barcelona match.

Messi has three sons. To celebrate Antonela's first pregnancy, he placed the ball under his shirt after scoring in Argentina's 4-0 win against Ecuador in June 2012. He later confirmed the pregnancy in an interview. His first son, named Thiago, was born in Barcelona on 2nd November 2012.

30th June 2017 a civil ceremony for Messi and Antonela was held at a luxury hotel in their home city of Rosario, Argentina. About 250 guests attended the wedding including Messi's Barcelona teammates Neymar, Cesc Fabregas, Luis Suárez, and Gerard Piqué. 150 journalists were allowed to cover the event but had no direct access to the ceremony or the wedding party.

In 2010, Messi became a UNICEF Children's

Ambassador. Immediately after his appointment, he traveled to Haiti to bring public awareness to the plight of the country's children in the wake of the earthquake. As part of his ongoing work for UNICEF, he has visited many countries all over the world to bring light to critical issues about children.

The Leo Messi Foundation was created in 2007. It is a non-profit organization set up to protect the health and safety of young children around the world who do not have the means to provide for themselves. It was born of the idea that all children should have the same opportunities to realize their dreams. In collaboration with other institutions, it carries out projects in line with the fundamental beliefs of the foundation, based on health, education, and sport.

Lionel Messi said about the foundation, "I reached my dream of becoming a footballer and I want you to know that I fought a lot to get there and I have to fight even more to stay. I want to take advantage of that effort and that success to help the children who need it the most, because that is how I have chosen it, I am moved every day that I get a child to smile when they think there is hope when I see that they feel happy. That is why we decided to create the Leo Messi Foundation. And I will continue fighting to make children happy with the same dedication that I need to continue being a footballer."

Messi has kept close ties to his roots in Argentina since he left Rosario at the age of 13. He still has the Rosario accent. He still owns the family's old house, though it has stayed uninhabited for many years. He owns an apartment for his mother and a family compound in the outskirts of the city. When on international duty he often travels back to Rosario to have dinner and spend the night with his family and a small group of confidants, most of whom were also part his boyhood club Newell's Old Boys "The Machine of 87".

Messi's professional affairs are mostly run like a family business, with his father acting as his agent since his move to Barcelona in 2000. His oldest brother Rodrigo, takes care of his publicity and daily schedules, while his mother and other brother Matias, handle his charitable organization, the Leo Messi Foundation, and also manage professional and personal matters in the family's hometown of Rosario in Argentina.

Messi loves tattoos. He has pictures of his relatives inked on his body. At first, he was too afraid of the pain and asked his wife Antonela to have one first. He and Antonela both have a tattoo of a crown on their arm. He also has a tattoo of Antonela's Eye, Jesus, a giant clock, a rosary, his mother's portrait, son's handprints, and on his left leg he has a ball and the number ten.

CHAPTER 10
RECORDS

I don't look at records, that's not why I'm playing the game. Goals, of course. Every player in my position wants to score goals. But most of all, trophies. My target is always to win trophies for Barcelona, and that will always be my motivation, to win things. Nothing feels better than doing that as a team.

- Leonel Messi

MESSI
10
unicef

TRIVIA QUESTIONS

1. **How many trophies in total has Messi won in his career?**
   a) 33
   b) 36
   c) 40
   d) 44

2. **How many times has Messi won the Ballon d'Or?**
   a) 5
   b) 6
   c) 7
   d) 8

3. **Messi holds the record for the most goals scored in El Classico matches. How many goals has scored?**
   a) 18
   b) 22
   c) 26
   d) 32

4. **In 2012, Messi broke the record for the most goals scored in a calendar year. How many goals did he score that year for club and country?**
   a) 71
   b) 81
   c) 91
   d) 101

5. **The most goals Messi scored against a single team was 38. Against which team was it?**
   a) Sevilla
   b) Atletico Madrid
   c) Valencia
   d) Athletic Club

6. **How many times was Messi La Liga's top goalscorer?**
   a) 6
   b) 8
   c) 10
   d) 12

7. **How many seasons did Messi win the European Golden Shoe competition?**
   a) 3
   b) 4
   c) 6
   d) 8

8. **Messi has the record for the most Liga hat-tricks. How many did he score?**
   a) 18
   b) 24
   c) 36
   d) 41

9. **Lionel Messi holds the record for most goals scored in Europe's top five leagues with how many goals?**
   a) 412
   b) 474
   c) 496
   d) 513

10. **Messi is the only player in history to score 40+ club goals in how many consecutive seasons?**
   a) 7
   b) 8
   c) 9
   d) 10

INTERACTIVE ACTIVITY CHALLENGE

Crossword 2

Answer the questions to complete the challenge

ACROSS

2. Inter Miami co-owner
4. Messi's World Cup
5. Messi's biggest influence
9. Barcelona vs Real Madrid
10. the number of son's Messi has

DOWN

1. Gave Messi his Barca debut
3. First trophy for Argentina
6. Argentina's World Cup Final opponents
7. Messi's number at Inter Miami
8. most goals scored in a year

ANSWERS

CHAPTER 10: RECORDS

TRIVIA QUESTIONS:

1. d) 44
2. c) 7
3. c) 26
4. c) 91
5. a) Sevilla
6. b) 8
7. c) 6
8. c) 36
9. c) 496
10. c) 9

INTERACTIVE ACTIVITY CHALLENGE: Cross Word 2

FUN FACTS, STOIRES AND STATS

Messi became the most decorated player in the history of the game when his new Inter Miami team beat Nashville SC in the Leagues Cup final. Over two decades, he has won a total of 44 trophies. 35 of which were won whilst at Barcelona, 3 in France with PSG, 5 with Argentina, and now one with Inter Miami.

Messi holds numerous La Liga records. He is the leagues top goal scorer with 474 goals. He has scored the most Liga hat-tricks with 36. He also holds the record for the most Liga titles won by a foreign player, with 10.

Messi is the leading goal scorer in the history of El Clasico matches. He scored 26 times during a glittering career with Barcelona. This included 18 goals in La Liga matches, six in the Supercopa, and two in the Champions League. Second on the list of scorers in the fixture is Real Madrid's hero Alfredo Di Stefano with 18, who held the record since his heyday in the 1960s. Also on 18 goals is Cristiano Ronaldo

Messi has won the Ballon d'Or a record Seven times. He finished third in 2007 behind Kaka and Cristiano Ronaldo. He finished second in 2008 behind Cristiano Ronaldo. He then won the converted prize Four times in a row between 2009 - 2012. Then again in 2015, 2019, and 2021.

Messi has never been known for his heading ability. In his 672 goals for Barcelona, he only scored 23 times with his head. He also didn't score a single goal for PSG with a header.

Messi won the European Golden Shoe six times. The winner is not only the player with the most goals scored in the season. There is a weighting system where the goals scored in the top-ranked leagues and competitions are worth more.

In 2012, Messi scored 91 goals for club and country, breaking the previous record of 85 held by Germany's Gerd Muller. He scored 79 times for Barcelona that year and 12 times for Argentina. The latter is an international record for his country.

As of November 2023, Messi has taken 133 penalties and scored 103 of them. That is a conversion rate of 79%. Only Cristiano Ronaldo has taken and scored more. He has so far taken 174 and scored 145. A conversion rate of 72%.

Messi is currently the most-capped Argentina player. As of 2023, he has played 174 times for his country and is one of just three players to have scored over 100 international goals for their country. The other two are Cristiano Ronaldo for Portugal and Ali Daei for Iran.

Messi holds the record for the most individual World Cup appearances. He represented Argentina 26 times in the competition. He has also scored the most goals for Argentina at a World Cup with 13. He is the only player to score in the World Cup group stages, the Round of 16, The Quarter-finals, the Semi-finals and the Final

I really hope you enjoyed MESSI: The Definitive Story of a Football Icon

Thanks so much for buying it and reading to the end

These books have been written with passion to help fans like you test and expand their knowledge of their favourite teams and players.

I would love you to help me spread the joy of this beautiful game by leaving an honest review on Amazon so other dedicated fans can enjoy the book aswell.

Its very simple

Scan the QR code and you'll be taken sraight to the review page

Thanks in advance!
Toby Everett

Made in United States
Orlando, FL
07 December 2023

40398401R00065